DETECTING DISASTERS

DETECTING
TORNADOES

by Marne Ventura

FOCUS
READERS

WWW.NORTHSTAREDITIONS.COM

Produced for North Star Editions by Red Line Editorial.

Photographs ©: Minerva Studio/Shutterstock Images, cover, 1; David R. Frazier/Science Source, 4–5; Justin Hobson/Shutterstock Images, 7; Martin Haas/Shutterstock Images, 9; Gary Hincks/Science Source, 10–11; Pavel Rahman/AP Images, 13; Kim Johnson Flodin/AP Images, 15; NOAA, 16–17; Bettmann/Getty Images, 18–19; Sue Ogrocki/AP Images, 21; Jamie Lusch/The Medford Mail Tribune/AP Images, 23; Jim Edds/Science Source, 24–25; Science Source, 27

Content Consultant: Paul Markowski, Professor of Meteorology, Penn State University

ISBN
978-1-63517-004-7 (hardcover)
978-1-63517-060-3 (paperback)
978-1-63517-166-2 (ebook pdf)
978-1-63517-116-7 (hosted ebook)

Library of Congress Control Number: 2016949763

Printed in the United States of America
Mankato, MN
November, 2016

ABOUT THE AUTHOR

Marne Ventura is the author of 41 books for kids. She loves writing about nature, science, technology, food, health, and crafts. She is a former elementary school teacher and holds a master's degree in education from the University of California.

TABLE OF CONTENTS

CHAPTER 1

TORNADO!

Mark Hardgrove peered out through the windshield of his car. It was January 2016. Heavy rain along the Florida highway made it hard to see. He slowed down. The windshield wipers swished back and forth. There was so much water on the road that he worried about losing control of his car.

Florida's frequent rainstorms can make driving dangerous and can lead to tornadoes.

He looked up at the western sky. Huge, dark, low clouds moved toward him. Mark had seen clouds like this before. They meant a tornado was coming.

Mark knew he needed to get out of the way. But there were cars on three sides of him. On the other side was the center divider of the highway. Mark was stuck. The sky darkened. The trees along the highway thrashed wildly.

The car started to rock back and forth. All at once, the windshield went dark as if it had been painted gray. Mark gripped the steering wheel as the tornado lifted his car into the air. The car somersaulted. Then it flipped back the other way.

Tornadoes are huge columns of powerful, swirling clouds.

Mark heard and felt a loud bang. He was on the ground again. Now he was stuck between his seat and the open air bag. Two truck drivers came to help. They popped the air bag with a pocketknife.

Mark's seat belt buckle was jammed shut. The men cut the strap so he could escape. They gave him water to drink.

Rescue workers took Mark to a hospital. He was treated for a broken finger. His only other injuries were bruises from the seat belt and sore arms from holding the steering wheel so tightly. He said his tornado experience felt like a bad, out-of-control amusement park ride.

TORNADOES BY STATE

Texas experiences the most US tornadoes. The state averaged 155 tornadoes per year from 1991–2000. Kansas came in second with an average of 96 per year during that time period. Florida averaged 66.

Tornadoes can easily toss cars around and damage buildings.

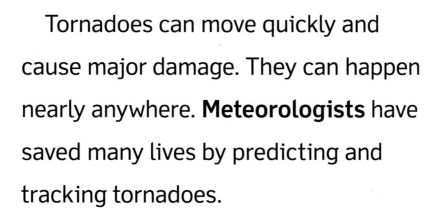

Tornadoes can move quickly and cause major damage. They can happen nearly anywhere. **Meteorologists** have saved many lives by predicting and tracking tornadoes.

CHAPTER 2

TORNADO SCIENCE

A tornado is a violently spinning **column** of air in contact with the ground. It is most often found beneath a thunderstorm. People also refer to tornadoes as twisters.

Scientists are still studying exactly how tornadoes form. However, they already know the basic ingredients.

Both rising, spinning warm air and sinking cool air are important for tornado formation.

Thunderstorms happen when warm, humid air near the ground has cooler air on top of it. The **temperature** of the air decreases rapidly with height. Meteorologists call this instability.

Tornadoes form within thunderstorms when instability is combined with large changes in wind speed or direction. These changes are known as wind shear. When temperature and wind speeds vary greatly with **altitude**, tornadoes are more likely to form.

Tornadoes can form almost anywhere in the world. Most happen in the central and southern plains of the United States. This area is sometimes called Tornado

A 1996 tornado in Bangladesh destroyed homes and killed more than 500 people.

Alley. There are an average of 1,200 tornadoes there yearly. After the United States, Argentina and Bangladesh are the countries with the next-highest numbers of tornadoes.

Tornado winds spin at speeds of up to 300 miles per hour (480 km/h). Tornadoes can travel along the ground at up to 60 miles per hour (97 km/h), and they can move dozens of miles from start to finish. Tornadoes can last from a few seconds to approximately an hour. Some tornadoes are strong enough to take

ENHANCED FUJITA SCALE

Meteorologists use the Enhanced Fujita (EF) scale to rate the power of a tornado. The scale ranges from 0 to 5. A twister that blows a few shingles off a roof is an EF-0. A severe tornado that destroys a house is an EF-5. The scale is named after storm researcher Tetsuya Fujita.

Tornadoes can rip through whole neighborhoods and cause widespread damage.

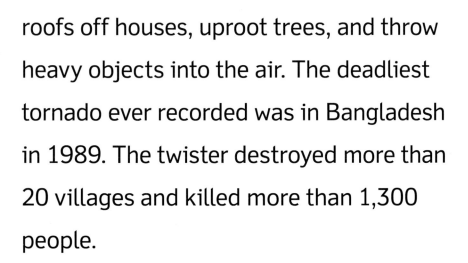

roofs off houses, uproot trees, and throw heavy objects into the air. The deadliest tornado ever recorded was in Bangladesh in 1989. The twister destroyed more than 20 villages and killed more than 1,300 people.

TORNADO ALLEY

Tornado Alley got its name in the 1950s, when US Air Force meteorologists launched a project called Tornado Alley to study twisters in the Midwest. The conditions in this region are ideal for large thunderstorms that can produce tornadoes. However, the borders of Tornado Alley are not clearly defined.

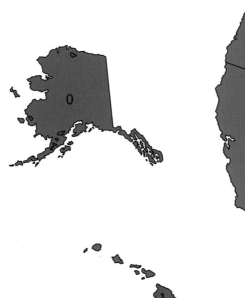

This map shows the average numbers of tornadoes per year in each state between 1991 and 2010. States that averaged 45 or more per year are shaded orange. The peak time of year for tornadoes in these areas is between May and June. They usually happen between 4:00 p.m. and 9:00 p.m.

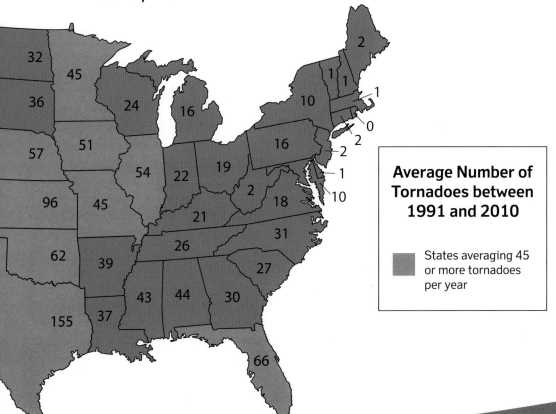

Average Number of Tornadoes between 1991 and 2010

States averaging 45 or more tornadoes per year

CHAPTER 3

TORNADO DETECTION

Little research on tornadoes was done before the 1880s. In 1882, US Army meteorologist John Park Finley made a list of rules for predicting tornadoes. But the rules were not given to the public. Army leaders did not want to scare people.

In the 1800s, relatively little was known about tornadoes or how to predict them.

The biggest development in tornado forecasting happened in 1948. US Air Force researchers studied the conditions that occurred before a tornado in Oklahoma. When they saw the same conditions appear a few days later, they predicted another tornado would form. They were correct.

In the 1950s, the public gained access to these forecasts. Meteorologists began warning the public when a tornado was predicted. These predictions became more accurate over time as scientists learned more about tornadoes.

Today, many meteorologists work for the National Weather Service.

Today's storm scientists use computers and other advanced tools to predict and track storms.

They alert people hours or even days before tornadoes will form.

Radar is an important tool for meteorologists. Energy is sent out from an **antenna**. When the energy strikes rain, some of the energy bounces back. The radar equipment senses the reflection.

Radars tell scientists the locations of storms and where they are moving to.

The government built a nationwide **Doppler radar** system in the United States to help track tornadoes and other severe weather. The system is known as NEXRAD.

WEATHER BALLOONS

The National Weather Service sends up 92 weather balloons twice a day, every day. The balloons stay in the air for approximately two hours. Instruments on the balloons measure temperature, **humidity**, and wind. This data is sent back to the National Weather Service. The information is fed into computers to improve storm predictions.

This NEXRAD radar site is on Mount Ashland in Oregon.

NEXRAD helped increase tornado warning times from 5 minutes to 13 minutes. This gave people in a tornado's path more time to seek shelter. The improvement has saved many lives.

CHAPTER 4

TORNADO SAFETY

The National Weather Service tells people when storms are coming. There are two types of notices about tornadoes. A tornado watch means current conditions might create a tornado. A tornado warning means a tornado has already been spotted or could form at any time.

Powerful sirens are used to warn people when a tornado has been spotted nearby.

People under a tornado watch must listen to the radio or television for more updates. They should be prepared to find shelter. People under a tornado warning must seek shelter immediately.

ADVANCE WARNING SAVES LIVES

In March 1925, a tornado created a path of destruction from Illinois to Indiana. Almost 700 people died because they did not have time to get to safety. In 1999, nearly 75 years later, a tornado hit central Oklahoma. Improvements in tornado detection made it possible to send out tornado warnings 30 minutes before the twister hit. This time, 44 people died. Without a warning, it could have been much worse. The alert saved many lives.

Decades of research have helped meteorologists learn more about tornadoes and how they form.

Houses in areas that are at risk for tornadoes often have storm cellars or basements. These are rooms built under the house. They are less likely to be damaged by a tornado's deadly winds.

People without storm cellars are safest if they stay on the lowest floor. They should be away from windows. An interior room, such as a walk-in closet, is a good choice.

Being prepared for a tornado is a smart idea. Listen for tornado watches and warnings. Thanks to the work of meteorologists, you'll have advance warning about these dangerous storms.

TORNADO SAFETY CHECKLIST

- Put together an emergency kit.

- Talk to your family about the safest place in your home to seek shelter from a tornado.

- If a storm is coming, listen to the radio or watch television for weather updates, tornado watches, and tornado warnings.

- Be aware of the signs of a tornado, including a dark and greenish sky, large hail, rotating clouds, and a loud roar that sounds like a train.

- If a tornado occurs when you are in a building, get to the basement or an interior room.

- Stay away from windows and outside walls.

- Get under a table or other sturdy object and cover your head and neck to stay safe from falling items.

- If you are in a mobile home and a tornado is coming, leave immediately and get to a safe shelter area in a nearby building.

- If you are outside with no shelter, find a low, flat location and watch out for flying debris.

FOCUS ON
DETECTING TORNADOES

Write your answers on a separate piece of paper.

1. Write a letter to a friend describing what you learned about tornado watches and tornado warnings.

2. If you had a choice of where to live, would you avoid areas with tornadoes? Why or why not?

3. Which US state experiences the most tornadoes?

   A. Florida
   B. Texas
   C. Illinois

4. Which type of notice is the most serious?

   A. tornado watch
   B. tornado alert
   C. tornado warning

Answer key on page 32.

GLOSSARY

altitude
Height above the ground.

antenna
A device for receiving and sending radio waves.

column
Something shaped like a tall, vertical tube.

Doppler radar
A tool that sends and receives energy waves to find storms and measure the winds inside them.

humidity
The amount of moisture in the air.

meteorologists
Scientists who study the weather.

temperature
How hot or cold something is.

TO LEARN MORE

BOOKS

Cernak, Linda. *The Science of a Tornado.* Ann Arbor, MI: Cherry Lake Publishing, 2016.

Fradin, Judith Bloom, and Dennis Brindell Fradin. *Tornado! The Story behind These Twisting, Turning, Spinning, and Spiraling Storms.* Washington, DC: National Geographic Kids, 2011.

O'Keefe, Emily. *Joplin Tornado Survival Stories.* Mankato, MN: The Child's World, 2016.

NOTE TO EDUCATORS

Visit **www.focusreaders.com** to find lesson plans, activities, links, and other resources related to this title.

INDEX

Answer Key: 1. Answers will vary; **2.** Answers will vary; **3.** B; **4.** C